Deep Dive

Level 6 – Orange

Helpful Hints for Reading at Home

The graphemes (written letters) and phonemes (units of sound) used throughout this series are aligned with Letters and Sounds. This offers a consistent approach to learning, whether reading at home or in the classroom.

HERE IS A LIST OF PHONEMES FOR THIS PHASE OF LEARNING. AN EXAMPLE OF THE PRONUNCIATION CAN BE FOUND IN BRACKETS.

Phase 5			
ay (day)	ou (out)	ie (tie)	ea (eat)
oy (boy)	ir (girl)	ue (blue)	aw (saw)
wh (when)	ph (photo)	ew (new)	oe (toe)
au (Paul)	a_e (make)	e_e (these)	i_e (like)
o_e (home)	u_e (rule, cube)		

Phase 5 Alternative Pronunciations of Graphemes			
a (hat, what)	e (bed, she)	i (fin, find)	o (hot, so, other)
u (but, unit)	c (cat, cent)	g (got, giant)	ow (cow, blow)
ie (tied, field)	ea (eat, bread)	er (farmer, herb)	ch (chin, school, chef)
y (yes, by, very)	ou (out, shoulder, could, you)		

HERE ARE SOME WORDS WHICH YOUR CHILD MAY FIND TRICKY.

Phase 5 Tricky Words			
oh	their	people	Mr
Mrs	looked	called	asked
could			

TOP TIPS FOR HELPING YOUR CHILD TO READ:

- Allow children time to break down unfamiliar words into units of sound and then encourage children to string these sounds together to create the word.

- Encourage your child to point out any focus phonics when they are used.

- Read through the book more than once to grow confidence.

- Ask simple questions about the text to assess understanding.

- Encourage children to use illustrations as prompts.

This book focuses on /i_e/ and /ie/ and is an Orange level 6 book band.

Can you fill in the gaps?

ti_e

mi_e

pi_e

sli_e

Answers: time, mice, pine, slice

Have you ever tried to dive? That is when you go down deep in the sea.

Divers can see sea life under the sea.
They have to look out for things with spikes
that can sting, such as sea urchins and starfish.

Crown-of-thorns starfish

Some divers can go deep, deep down.
The air from a tank keeps them alive.

First, divers get dressed in their gear. They connect their air tanks with a pipe. They check it all a few times as they need to be safe.

Then, they ride a boat to a good spot to dive. To get off the boat in a deep spot, they do a stride dive and just step off the boat.

Stride dive

They can do a back roll from the boat when they are in a spot that is not deep.

Back roll

Divers cannot speak or hear under the sea.

To say something, divers need their hands. A ring with three fingers up tells people they are fine.

It is quite dark deep under the sea, as the sunlight cannot reach there. Divers bring lights with them that can shine under the sea.

Dive light

In order to be safe, divers take a long time to come up from the sea.

Divers can look for sharks under the sea. They stay inside a metal pen with thick bars so that they do not get hurt.

The sharks cannot bite them there.

©2023 **BookLife Publishing Ltd.**
King's Lynn, Norfolk, PE30 4LS, UK

ISBN 978-1-80505-080-3

All rights reserved. Printed in China.
A catalogue record for this book is
available from the British Library.

Deep Dive
Written by Charis Mather
Designed by Danielle Rippengill

MIX
Paper from responsible sources
FSC® C113515

An Introduction to BookLife Readers...

Our Readers have been specifically created in line with the London Institute of Education's approach to book banding and are phonetically decodable and ordered to support each phase of the Letters and Sounds document.

Each book has been created to provide the best possible reading and learning experience. Our aim is to share our love of books with children, providing both emerging readers and prolific page-turners with beautiful books that are guaranteed to provoke interest and learning, regardless of ability.

BOOK BAND GRADED using the Institute of Education's approach to levelling.

PHONETICALLY DECODABLE supporting each phase of Letters and Sounds.

EXERCISES AND QUESTIONS to offer reinforcement and to ascertain comprehension.

CLEAR DESIGN to inspire and provoke engagement, providing the reader with clear visual representations of each non-fiction topic.

AUTHOR INSIGHT:
CHARIS MATHER

Charis Mather is a children's author at BookLife Publishing who has a love for reading and writing. Her studies in linguistics and experiences working with young readers have given her a knack for writing material that suits a range of ages and skill levels. Charis is passionate about producing books that emphasise the fun in reading and is convinced that no matter how much you already know, there is always something new to learn.

PHASE 5 /i_e/ /ie/

This book focuses on /i_e/ and /ie/ and is an Orange level 6 book band.

Image Credits Images are courtesy of Shutterstock.com. With thanks to Getty Images, Thinkstock Photo and iStockphoto. Cover – dibrova, Magicleaf, Solarisys. p2–3 – Photoonlife, Eric Isselee, My Sunnyday, bestv. p4–5 – ChameleonsEye, Max Topchii, Richard Whitcombe. p6–7 – Photos BrianScantlebury, Stas Moroz. p8–9 – U.S. Navy photo by Mass Communication Specialist 2nd Class Justin Stumberg, Public domain, via Wikimedia Commons, Widhibek. p10–11 – Dudarev Mikhail, Rich Carey. p12–13 – frantisekhojdysz, Lilllac. p14–15 – VisionDive.